I See! I See!

by Myles Rijada
illustrated by Stephen Lewis

Scott Foresman

Editorial Offices: Glenview, Illinois • New York, New York
Sales Offices: Reading, Massachusetts • Duluth, Georgia
Glenview, Illinois • Carrollton, Texas • Menlo Park, California

I see a monkey.

I see a .

I see a .

I see a .
bear

I see a tiger.

I see a .

I see me!